KU-376-437

BRITAIN SINCE 1930

Rosemary Rees
Sue Styles
Christa Hook

HEINEMANN
EDUCATIONAL

Heinemann Educational
a division of Heinemann Publishers (Oxford) Ltd
Halley Court, Jordan Hill, Oxford OX2 8EJ

OXFORD LONDON EDINBURGH MADRID
ATHENS BOLOGNA PARIS MELBOURNE
SYDNEY AUCKLAND SINGAPORE TOKYO
IBADAN NAIROBI HARARE GABORONE
PORTSMOUTH NH (USA)

© Rosemary Rees, Sue Styles, Christa Hook

The moral right of the proprietors has been
asserted

First published 1992

**British Library Cataloguing in Publication
Data** is available from the British Library on
request.

ISBN 0 435 31808 X

Designed by Ron Kamen, Green Door Design
Ltd, Basingstoke, Hants

Printed in Spain by Mateu Cromo

Acknowledgements
The authors and publisher would like to thank
the following for permission to reproduce
photographs:

Barnaby's Picture Library: 8E, 9Q, 10D, 10M
Bodleian Library: 9G
British Airways/Adrian Meredith: 10K, 10O
Camera Press: 5B
Cinema Bookshop/Ronald Grant: 9J
Environmental Picture Library: 10E
Mary Evans Picture Library: 2w0
John Frost Historical Newspaper Service: 3G, 9L
John Frost Historical Newspaper Service/Val
Randall: 1E
The Girl Guide Association: 2wK, 9S
Greater London Photograph Library: 3D
Harlow Study & Visitors' Centre: 3B, 3C, 7B,
Hulton Deutsch Collection Ltd: 1F, 1J, 1M, 2wA,
2wF, 2wL, 2wM, 2pA, 6H, 9K, 10N
The Labour Party: 2pC
Leeds Design Consultancy: 7D
London Transport Museum: 10F
Magnum/Peter Manow: 6G
National Motor Museum, Beaulieu: 3F
The *Observer*: 6K
Robert Opie Collection: 1A, 2wI, 2wJ, 5J, 6E, 9A,
9B, 9C, 9P, 10G
Philip Parkhouse: 7A, 9H
Picturepoint Ltd: 8A
Popperfoto: 3H, 4D, 4F, 4H, 4J, 7C,
Jill Posener: 5I
Private Collection: 8B
Quadrant Picture Library: 10I, 10J
Raleigh: 9R
Redferns/M. Cameron: 6J
Roger-Viollet: 8C
Sony UK: 9N
Alan Thomas: 4A, 4C
Topham Picture Source: 1C, 1D, 1G, 2wC, 2pD,
2pE, 2pF, 4E, 4I, 5E, 6B, 6F, 8D, 9D, 9I, 9M, 9O,
10A, 10B, 10C, 10H, 10P
The Vintage Magazine Co: 9E
Source H on page 53 is reproduced
by permission of Penguin Books Ltd

Cover photograph: Topham Picture Source.

Every effort has been made to contact copyright
holders of material reproduced in this book. Any
omissions will be rectified in subsequent
printings if notice is given to the publisher.

CONTENTS

1 The Thirties: rich and poor

It is summer 1936. Stan and May Williams have been married for a year. They live in a new house in Barnehurst, Kent. Stan works for the General Post Office at its London headquarters. He goes to work each day by train. May does not go out to work. Stan does not want her to. He earns £5 a week, which is more than enough to keep them both.

Stan and May get up early. Stan has to catch the 7.35 am train to London. He has quite a long walk to the station, so he must not be late leaving home. This morning a letter arrived while May was frying eggs and bacon for Stan's breakfast. The letter is from Stan's cousin, Harry. Harry lives in Jarrow, a town in the north east of England. Harry writes that he is going to join a march to London. 'What is this all about?' Stan wonders.

Source A

Thousands of new houses were built in the 1930s. This is an advertisement for some which were built in Barnehurst, Kent.

May got up extra early today so that she could make a start on the washing. It is Monday, and Monday is wash day. It is raining, which means she will have to dry everything indoors. May cooks, cleans, bakes, sews, washes, irons and does the shopping. She keeps the flowerbeds in the garden tidy, but Stan mows the grass. She makes jam and pickles. She bottles the fruit and vegetables which Stan grows on his allotment. May wants Stan to buy her one of the new electric vacuum cleaners. He has just had a pay rise. Perhaps this year they will have a summer holiday in a hotel in Eastbourne or even Torquay.

The Williams Family

In this book you will read about the Williams family. You will also see pictures of them. They are not a real family. However, their lives are like the lives of ordinary people who lived in Britain between 1930 and 1980.

Stan and May in their kitchen.

Only rich parents could afford to send their sons to public schools. Often these boys went on to the universities of Oxford or Cambridge. Most of them got top jobs. They became lawyers, politicians, doctors, big businessmen and leaders of industry.

Girls from rich families usually went to expensive private schools. When most rich girls were about 18 they went to Buckingham Palace and met the King and Queen. They went to lots of dances. Their parents expected them to marry boys from rich families. Rich people owned over half the wealth of Britain.

Ordinary people did get to the top. A man called Ramsay MacDonald came from a poor family living in a Scottish fishing village. In the 1930s he was Prime Minister twice.

Source C

Visitors to Lords cricket ground, in London, on 9 July 1937. They were going to watch a match between boys from two public schools, Eton and Harrow.

Source D

Only rich people could afford to go fox hunting.

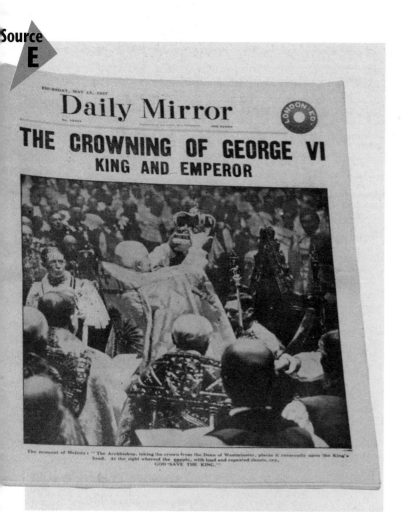

Daily Mirror

THURSDAY, MAY 13, 1937

THE CROWNING OF GEORGE VI
KING AND EMPEROR

The moment of Majesty: "The Archbishop, taking the crown from the Dean of Westminster, places it reverently upon the King's head. At the sight whereof the people, with loud and repeated shouts, cry, GOD 'SAVE THE KING.'"

A newspaper photograph of King George VI being crowned in Westminster Abbey on 12 May 1937. Thousands of people like Stan and May went to London and stood in the rain to cheer their new King.

In January 1936 King George V died. His eldest son was **proclaimed** King Edward VIII. King Edward wanted to marry an American, Wallis Simpson. Mrs Simpson had been married and divorced twice before. This meant that they could not be married in the Church of England. Mrs Simpson could not be crowned Queen of England.

In December 1936 King Edward decided to **abdicate**. He said his younger brother was to be king instead of him. Many people were shocked. Some said Edward should be allowed to marry Mrs Simpson and be king as well. Some said he should give up Mrs Simpson and stay king.

On 12 May 1937 Edward's younger brother was crowned King George VI. A month later Edward and Mrs Simpson got married. A new title was invented for them: the Duke and Duchess of Windsor.

Activities

1 Look at Sources C and D. List as many things as you can which tell you that these are rich people.

2 a Draw a picture or write a paragraph to show what you think rich people look like today.
   b Are they different from the people you can see in Sources C and D?

3 Look at Source E.
   a Find the King in this photograph. How do you know it is the King?
   b Who do you think all the other people are?

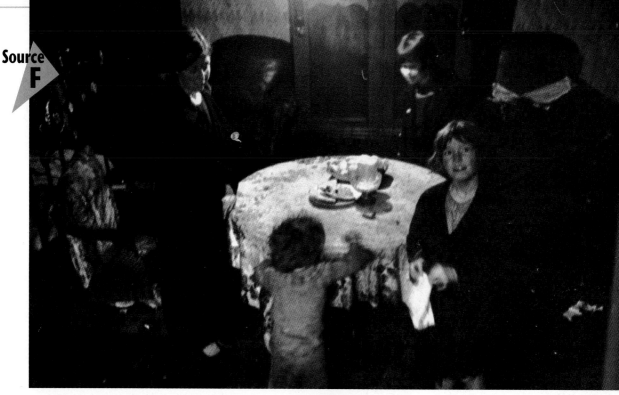

This family lived in one room in a house in Newcastle. All the food they had is on the table. The photo was taken in December 1938.

Couples like Stan and May weren't very rich but millions of people were poorer than them. Sometimes poor families lived in one room. They cooked, ate, washed and slept there. They did not have a bathroom. They washed in a basin or tin bath in front of the fire. They did not have an inside toilet. They had to go to an outside lavatory which was used by as many as 20 other people. Their houses did not have electricity. Their lights were gas lights or oil lamps. They cooked on a wood or coal fire, which also warmed the room.

Between April 1934 and March 1939 **local councils** had over 250,000 **slum** houses like these pulled down. More than a million people were offered new houses or flats to rent.

These new council flats were built in Wapping, East London, in the 1930s.

Unemployment was high in the 1930s. Everyone was afraid of being out of work. In the First World War (1914–18) many people worked in industries like ship building, coal mining and iron and steel making. These industries were in the north of England, southern Scotland, south Wales and Northern Ireland. Once the war was over these jobs disappeared. Hundreds of thousands of people were out of work. Some got jobs in new industries like electricity and car-making. These industries were in the Midlands and south-east England. But many could find no work at all. In 1933 nearly three million people were unemployed.

Workers took wage cuts rather than lose their jobs. Often they had such low wages that they could not afford to feed or clothe their families.

Source I

If there was a vacancy in the warehouse there would be as many as 100 men applying for it. I've seen men weep because they were out of work.

A retired West Yorkshire mill worker remembers in the 1980s what life was like in the 1930s.

Activities

1 Look at Source F.
   Find as many things as you can which tell you that these were poor people.

2 Look at Source G.
   These flats were built in the 1930s. Do you think they were built for rich or poor people? Why do you think this?

3 The figures in Source H show you how many people were out of work between 1928 and 1938.
   a Use these figures to make a bar-chart.
   b In which year were **most** people out of work? How many was this?
   c In which year were **fewest** people out of work? How many was this?

Source H

Unemployment 1928–1938	
1928	1.25 million
1930	1.75 million
1932	2.80 million
1934	2.25 million
1936	1.75 million
1938	1.80 million

Unemployment 1928–1938.

Life was hard for people who were unemployed. The government insurance scheme paid them some money for 26 weeks. Hundreds of thousands of people could not find work in 26 weeks. The government paid these people money which everyone called **the dole**. People only got dole money if government officials decided that they really needed it. These officials added up all the money coming in to a family. Even 3d a week from a son or daughter's paper round counted. Then the father's dole money was worked out. This was called the **means test**. Unemployed people hated officials asking about their family affairs. Most of the time they did not argue, because without the dole they would starve. Sometimes they organized **hunger marches** to show the rest of the country what was happening to them.

Source J

An unemployed man in Wigan, in 1933.

Source K

Mrs J's husband had been out of work for 14 weeks. Though she was breast feeding the baby, I found that all the food she herself had had yesterday was a cup of tea at breakfast time, and tea and two slices of bread and butter, provided by a married sister living near, at tea time. From the husband's unemployment pay of £1 0s 0d a week, 5s had to go to pay off a debt, 6s 3d for rent and only 8s 9d was left for food and fire.

A Health Visitor wrote this in the 1930s after one of her visits to a poor family. (Look at the Conversion Chart on page 64 to see what these amounts would be in modern money.)

Source L

Nothing to do with time; nothing to spend; nothing to do tomorrow nor the day after; nothing to wear; can't get married.

One of the characters in a novel called 'Love on the Dole' explains what it was like to be unemployed. This book was published in 1933.

Activities

Look carefully at Source J. Think of a title for the photograph. Try to find one word which describes really well what you can see in the photograph.

Hunger marchers from Jarrow on their way to London in 1936.

Jarrow was a ship-building town in the north-east of England. In 1936 eighty out of every hundred men in Jarrow were unemployed. Two hundred of these unemployed men marched to London. Men like Stan's brother Harry joined the march. They wanted to show the rest of the country how much they needed work. Kind people gave them food when they stopped to rest on their way to London. Bishops blessed them. The Leicester Co-op mended their boots. The government in London did nothing to help them. When the men got back home they found that their dole money had been cut. The people of Jarrow did not begin working again until the shipyards began building warships to fight in the Second World War (1939–45).

How do we know about the past?

1 Draw two columns, headed: **source** and **answer**. For each of the questions below, decide which source gives you the answer. Write the source letter in the **source** column. Then put your answer in the **answer** column.

Question	Source	Answer
Who was crowned King in May 1937?		
How many people were unemployed in 1934?		
When was the Jarrow March?		

2 You are writing for an important newspaper in 1938. You are looking back at the 1930s. The title of your article is 'Rich and Poor in the 1930s'. Use the sources in this Unit to help you to write all about this.

2 The Forties: war and peace

War

It is April 1941. May, her baby Janet, her mum Ethel, her brother Jack and Rags the dog are all squashed into the Anderson shelter in Stan and May's garden. They have been there for two hours. They can hear the drone of German bombers overhead. Sometimes the ground shakes as a bomb lands near them. They hope they will be safe. They hope Stan and May's house will not be hit. Fred, May's dad, stayed in the house when the air-raid sirens sounded the alarm. He got into the cupboard under the stairs. He thought he would be safer there.

Stan joined the army in 1939 when war broke out. He is fighting in the deserts of north Africa. Stan hasn't seen his daughter Janet yet. May is doing her bit, too. She joined the WVS (Women's Voluntary Service) in 1939 and helps people who have been bombed out of their homes. Her neighbour Ruby is working in a munitions factory.

Jack isn't allowed to leave his job and fight in the war. This is because the work he is doing is important, and may help Britain win the war. He works in a factory which makes ships' engines.

They all hope the raid will be over soon. They can then see what damage has been done and whether any friends or neighbours have been hurt or killed.

Source A

People took cover in Anderson Shelters to protect themselves against air raids.

Activities

1 Look at Source B.
  a Can you find:
     May and Janet?
     May's mum, Ethel?
     May's brother Jack?
     Rags the dog?
  b Can you see:
     Stan's photograph?
     Janet's gas-mask?
     a ration book?

2 Why was Stan not in the shelter?

3 Why was Jack not away fighting?

May and her family in their
Anderson shelter.

On 3 September 1939 people heard on the wireless that Great Britain was at war with Germany. Millions of people, like Stan, went to fight. Thousands of women were left to cope alone. They had to keep their families safe and well for as long as the war lasted.

The Germans bombed British towns and cities. The worst bombing was called the '**Blitz**'. It happened between September 1940 and May 1941. German bombers attacked London and other important towns like Coventry, Birmingham, Hull, Sheffield, Southampton, Manchester, Cardiff, Belfast, Plymouth and Bristol. The bombers usually came by night, when there was a '**bombers' moon**' for the pilots to see by. They sometimes made **daylight raids** as well.

Air Raid Precaution (ARP) wardens looked after people during and after air-raids. They called ambulances and fire engines. They helped dig people out of their homes. They made sure, too, that there was a **blackout** at night. Not a chink of light must be seen. Enemy planes must not be given a clue as to where to drop their bombs.

Many families had their own air-raid shelters. Public shelters were built in cities and towns for everyone to use. Some factories and offices built their own shelters. In London people slept at night in deep Underground railway stations. Everyone had a **gas mask** in case the Germans dropped gas bombs, but they never did.

Source C

The Elephant and Castle Underground station during the Blitz, 11 November 1940.

Source D

We didn't notice the war, really. The only bit of excitement was when a bomb dropped on Eldroth moor and killed five sheep.

Mrs Morphet from Yorkshire remembers in the 1980s what life was like during the war.

Source E

The hours dragged on as we waited for the inevitable bomb. The throb of the German planes, the bells of the fire engines. We were too frightened to move. Four adults, one baby, one dog. We huddled together waiting for death.

Jean Long remembers an air-raid on Coventry.

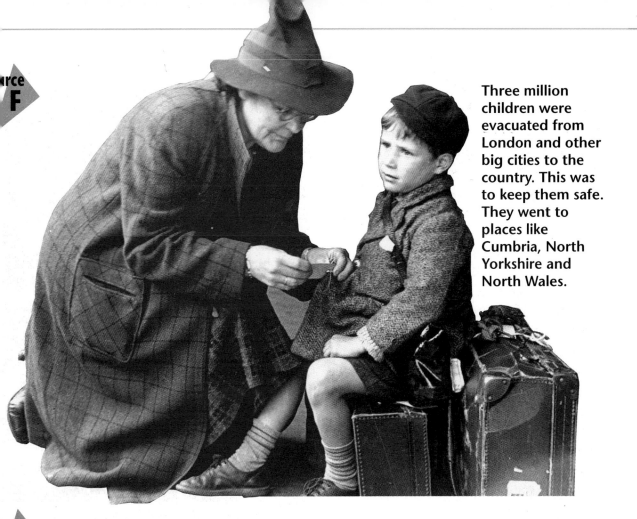

Source F

Three million children were evacuated from London and other big cities to the country. This was to keep them safe. They went to places like Cumbria, North Yorkshire and North Wales.

Source G

Everything was so clean. We were given face flannels and tooth brushes. We'd never cleaned our teeth until then. Hot water came from the tap, and there was a lavatory upstairs. This was all very odd. I didn't like it.

A boy, aged 13, writes about his evacuation.

Source H

Evacuation was the most exciting thing that happened to me. After school we were expected to work, sweeping out Mr Benson's butcher's shop. At home I never helped Father at his bank! In Settle I played in the fields and on the moors with village boys.

A boy, aged 13, writes about his evacuation from Bradford to Settle, in North Yorkshire, when he was 9 years old.

Activities

1 Look at Source C.
Make a list of all the problems you can think of about sleeping in an Underground station. Can you think of any good things about being there?

2 Do you think that people like May and her family would have liked to be in an Underground station during the war instead of their Anderson shelter?

3 Look at Source F. Read Sources G and H. Write a letter about a little boy or girl who was evacuated during the war. If you like, it could be the boy in Source F.

Enemy submarines sank cargo ships bringing goods like beef, lamb, butter, wheat, oranges and bananas to Britain. The government rationed food to make sure the people didn't starve. Everyone had a **ration book** full of **coupons**. These coupons as well as money, had to be given to shopkeepers, for eggs, jam, cheese, butter, meat, bacon, milk, sugar, sweets, tea and soap. Some people were allowed more than others. Pregnant women had green ration books and got the first choice of any fruit and twice the egg ration. Children had blue ration books. They were allowed fruit, when the shops had any, and half a pint of milk a week. As well as coupons, everybody had 16 **points** a month to 'spend' as they liked on scarce food like tinned fish and macaroni. People got used to empty shelves and to queuing for everything.

People grew fruit and vegetables to help feed themselves and their families. Some of them had allotments. Others only had window boxes. Local councils dug up parks and playing fields. They planted cabbages, parsnips, potatoes, leeks and carrots. The government called this '**Digging for Victory**', and asked everyone to help.

Source I

Give yourself a HAPPY HOLIDAY.

...and help our farmers.

LEND A HAND ON THE LAN

AT AN AGRICULTURAL CA

Farmers ploughed as much land and produced as much food as they could. They needed help to do this, especially at harvest time. Many people from towns and cities had farming holidays.

Source J

A typical week's supply of rationed food for one adult. Food was rationed differently at different times, depending on supplies.

A lot of things which people threw out as rubbish before the war were saved and re-cycled in the 1940s. Here, Girl Guides are collecting jam jars, rags, tins and paper.

Women like May tried to **make do and mend** during the war years. Clothes, towels, sheets, blankets and curtains were rationed. Everything unwanted or worn out was made into something else. They turned old sheets into baby clothes, net curtains into a wedding dress, flour sacks into chair covers and worn out trousers into girls' skirts. Nothing was wasted. They cut up old stockings and socks and used them as stuffing for pillows and soft toys.

Many people bought things on the **black market.** There was always someone who knew a man who would sell petrol, eggs, spare parts for a radio, toys or alcohol on the quiet. '**Spivs**' and '**wideboys**' ignored government regulations and sold whatever they could get hold of. Sometimes organized gangs stole goods from warehouses. Sometimes people **looted** bombed houses or shops, and kept or sold what they found there.

Activities

1 The war caused many problems. Here are some of the people who tried to help solve them. What did each group of people do?

  • the British government
  • local councils
  • farmers
  • Girl Guides
  • women, like May

2 Can you think of any other problems? What might people have done to help with these?

In May 1940 the German army reached the English Channel. People were very afraid that the Germans would cross the sea and **invade** Britain. The government told people to put huge concrete blocks and coils of barbed wire on the beaches. They told people to build look-out posts, called **pill-boxes**, along the cliffs. Farmers parked old tractors and ploughs in open fields to stop gliders landing. Vicars stopped ringing church bells on Sundays. Everyone agreed that church bells would only be rung to warn people that the Germans were invading.

Everybody got ready for an invasion, not just people living near the south and east coasts. Men who were not in the forces joined the **Local Defence Volunteers**, which was soon called the **Home Guard**. They trained to fight back invading troops. Women were not allowed to join. They formed the **Women's Home Defence Corps** instead, and learned to fire rifles and pistols too.

Source L

Local Home Guard practising. At first they did not have proper uniforms or rifles. This photo was taken in 1940.

Source M

Sign posts were taken away from road junctions so that invading Germans would get lost.

Source N

We shall defend our island whatever the cost may be. We shall fight on the beaches, we shall fight on the landing grounds, we shall fight in the fields and in the streets, we shall fight in the hills. We shall never surrender.

Winston Churchill, the Prime Minister, said this on 4 June 1940.

CARELESS TALK
COSTS LIVES

You never know who's listening!

The government was afraid that people might give away secrets without meaning to. They published a series of posters called 'Careless Talk Costs Lives'. This one shows Hitler, the German dictator, and Goering, the chief of the German airforce, sitting behind two women who are gossiping on a bus.

What do people say about the past?

1 Who are the real people in this list?

King George VI and Queen Elizabeth
May and Stan Williams
The Girl Guides in Source K (page 17)
The two men in Source O (page 19)
The two women in Source O (page 19)

2 Mrs Jones and Mr Smith are teachers. They are planning a lesson for their classes on what happened in Britain during the war.

'I shall tell the children that the war began in September 1939. I shall say how hard it was for people at home in Britain during the war. Their houses were bombed. They were short of food.'

What differences can you find between what Mrs Jones and Mr Smith are saying?

3 Mrs Jones and Mr Smith are both giving their **points of view** about the war. They are also giving **facts**. Find one **fact** and one **point of view** in what each teacher is saying.

'I shall tell the children that some people had a good time in the war. Some places were not bombed. Some people were not short of food.'

Peace

Hector comes home at the end of the war.

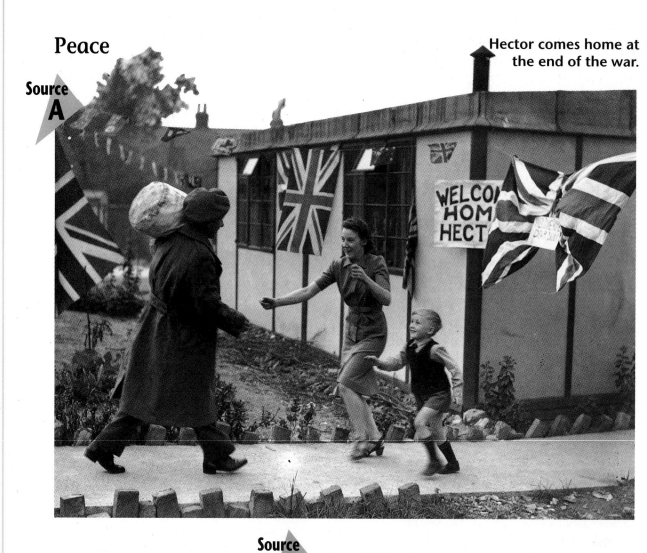

WELCOM
HOM
HECT

On 8 May 1945 the war in Europe ended. People hung up flags and banners. They sang, danced and had parties in the streets. Some parties were specially for the children. The grown-ups put tables in the road. They made cakes, buns and jellies. They cut sandwiches and blew up balloons. Everyone was happy because the war was over.

For some families the end of the war was a sad time. People they loved had been killed and would never come home.

6 June 1944	Invasion started in France at dawn. Did fractions – got on all right.
7 June	Went to Brownies. Had my bike out.
12 June	Mr Churchill went over to France. Mum not very well. Did biking.
19 June	Went to bed under the table. No warnings in the night. Can get off my bike properly.
22 June	Went to bed under the table. Eight warnings in the night.
19 July	Went to school. Warning went.
27 April 1945	Linked up with Russians. Had netball.
8 May	War over. Victory. Flag up. Bonfire.
12 May	Victory party in street.

Part of the diary of a ten-year-old schoolgirl, June 1944 – May 1945.

On 5 July 1945 there was a **General Election**. People voted for the **party** they wanted to govern Britain for the next five years.

The **Labour Party**, and their leader **Clement Attlee**, made lots of promises. They said there would never again be as many unemployed people as there were in the 1930s. They promised to build new houses for people who needed them. They promised to **nationalize** important industries and run them for the good of everybody. They promised to set up a **National Health Service** which would give everybody free medical treatment.

Many people thought the **Conservative Party**, and their leader **Winston Churchill**, would win the election. Churchill had led the British people through the war. Surely the people would want him to lead them in the peace which followed? A lot of people, however, remembered the unemployment of the 1930s. They remembered, too, that Britain wasn't really ready to fight a war in 1939. They blamed the Conservative Party.

Many people voted Labour in 1945 for the first time. The Labour Party won more seats in the **House of Commons** than any other party. There was a **Labour government**. Clement Attlee was **Prime Minister**. Most people thought the Labour Party would make the sort of Britain they wanted to live in.

Source C

THIS IS OUR CHANCE TO...

LABOUR

FOR HIM

VOTE LABOUR AND WIN THE PEACE!

LABOUR X

The Labour Party used this poster in 1945 to try to persuade people to vote for them.

Activities

1 Find an important event for each of these dates:

   June 6, 1944
   May 8, 1945
   July 5, 1945

2 Look at Source A. Write a poem or a story which tells how one of the people in the photograph felt when Hector came home.

In 1945 Britain was in a bad way. There were shops, offices, factories and houses in ruins. Docks were destroyed. Roads and railways were worn out. All these had to be rebuilt. The government had borrowed millions of pounds from other countries to help pay for the war. Now the money had to be paid back. To do this factories had to work again and make goods for **export**.

The Morris Cowley car factory in Oxford, in 1946. It aimed to produce 2,500 cars a week.

The new Labour government was very strict. They said car makers could only have steel if they made cars for export. They told new factories to open where there were lots of people out of work. They ordered **oil refineries** to be built. These refineries made petrol out of Arab oil, which was cheaper than USA oil. Refineries also provided raw material to make man-made fibres like **nylon**, **rayon** and **terylene**.

The Labour government believed that some industries were too important to be owned by individuals. They said that coal, iron, steel, electricity, gas and the railways should be run by the state. They **nationalized** all these industries. The government tried to make sure they were modernized and run efficiently.

More than 60,000 houses were built from 1945–46. Among them were 40,000 'pre-fabs' like these.

The Labour government said that it was their job to see that every man, woman and child in Britain was properly looked after. They ordered council houses and whole new towns to be built. They started a **National Health Service**, which gave free treatment to everyone. This was the beginning of the **Welfare State**.

Factories were rebuilt. Goods worth millions of pounds were exported. Money owed to other countries was paid back. There was very little unemployment. People earned good wages. There was, however, a problem. People had suffered a lot during the war. There had not been enough food, fuel or clothing. After the war rationing carried on. Even bread was rationed in 1946, something which had not happened during the war. Many people did not understand why. They saw goods they wanted to buy being exported to other countries. The terrible winter of 1947 did not help. Many people could not buy enough coal or food to keep themselves warm. In the General Election of 1950 the Labour government had a majority of just eight seats. There was another General Election in 1951 which the Conservatives won.

Activities

After the war some things were good and some were bad. Read pages 22 and 23 again. Look at Sources D, E and F. Write down a list of **good** things and a list of **bad** things.

Were things different then?

1 Look at Source F on page 23.
Why do you think the farmer is using horses to pull the plough and not a tractor?

2 Look at Source H on page 9. How many people were out of work during the 1930s?
Now read page 23 again. Were as many people out of work during the 1940s?

3 Make a picture showing the happy things which happened to people after the war was over. You could draw:
• victory bonfires
• soldiers coming home
• new houses (like prefabs)

urce
F

Ploughing during the terrible winter of 1947.

3 The fantastic Fifties

It is 2 June 1953. There are a lot of people in Stan and May's front room. They are all watching television. Stan has hired a set so that his family can watch the Coronation of Queen Elizabeth II. Not many people in their street have a TV. Jim and Ruby from next door, with their children Barry, Susan and Sheila have come to watch the Coronation too.

May has made tea and cut sandwiches for them all. Robert is already half-way through a bottle of ginger beer. Janet is thirteen now and goes to the girls' grammar school. She hopes the younger children will keep quiet. She doesn't want to miss anything. Her baby sister Alison will soon be asleep on Mum's lap, but Robert is six and can be very noisy. She saw Dad put a pile of comics – *Tiny Tots*, *Beano* and *Dandy* – behind his chair. Those will keep the younger ones quiet!

Source A

May hopes Stan will decide to buy the TV. There are some good programmes, like *Muffin the Mule* and *The Secret Garden* which Robert and Janet would enjoy. Stan would like the sport on Saturday afternoons. She would like to watch some of those new cookery programmes. A lot of food is not rationed any more. It would be fun to try new recipes.

Activities

Look at Source A. Two families are watching the Coronation in Stan and May's house. Can you find:

a May and Stan
Janet, their elder daughter
Robert, their son
Alison, their baby daughter

b Ruby and Jim
Susan and Sheila, their daughters
Barry, their son

The Williams family and friends watching the Coronation on TV.

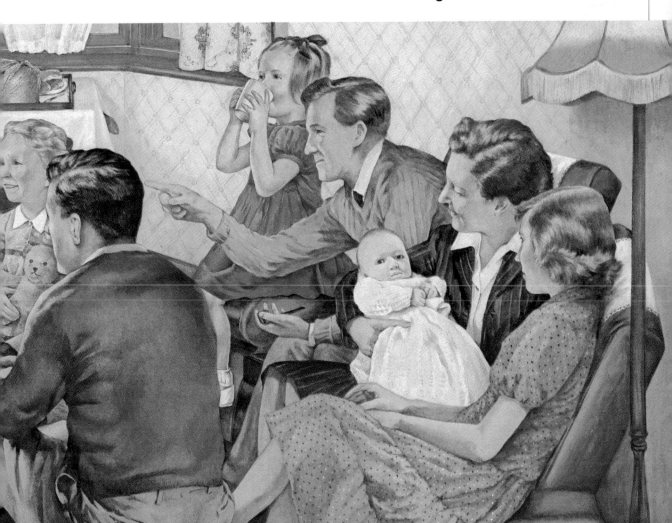

People desperately needed new homes. Houses were destroyed during the war. People were living in pre-fabs or with relatives. Many more were living in **slums**. The government, local councils and private builders worked hard. One plan was to build whole new cities out in the countryside. Jobs, schools and shops would be within easy reach of people's homes. Twenty new towns were built by 1961. People moved into them from the cities.

Shopping began to change. Usually people went to the baker for bread, the butcher for meat, the greengrocer for fruit and vegetables and the fishmonger for fish. Every shop had shop assistants who got the customers what they wanted. However, in 1950 the first **self-service** shop in Britain opened in Croydon. By the end of the 1950s, most large towns had a **supermarket**.

Source C

This is a kitchen in a house in Harlow, Essex, which was one of the new towns. This photograph was taken in 1957.

Source B

These are some of the new shops which were built in Harlow. This photograph was taken in 1953.

In 1944 Parliament made a law about children and schools. This law said that all children had to leave primary school when they were eleven. Then they had to go to a secondary school until they were at least fifteen. This would not cost their parents anything. Schools provided free milk at playtime. They had to provide lunches for everyone who wanted them.

Most children took an examination just before they finished primary school. This decided what sort of secondary school they went to. Some children were good at practical subjects. These children went to **secondary modern** school. Children who were good at subjects which needed a lot of reading and writing went to **grammar** school. About one child in every five went to grammar school.

Source D

This is a London primary school in 1958. Lots of new primary schools were built in the 1950s. Thousands more babies than usual were born after the end of the Second World War. This was called a baby-boom. Children like Robert were part of the baby-boom. By the 1950s all these children were old enough to go to school. New schools were built for them.

Source E

One summer holiday a lot of children got polio. Some were paralysed and some died. The council closed all the public swimming baths. They thought children caught polio at the baths. I remember cycling to our doctor's surgery. He gave me my first injection against polio. All my friends had injections too. It didn't cost anything. It was free because of the National Health Service.

Rosemary Dawson remembers the 1950s.

Activities

1 a Look at Source C. Is this like your kitchen? If not, how is it different?

   b Now look back at the picture of Stan and May's kitchen on page 5.
      Make a list of all the things which are different from the kitchen in Source C.
      Make a list of all the things which are similar to the kitchen in Source C.

2 Draw a picture of what your school looks like from the outside. Does it look like the school in Source D? How is it similar? How is it different?

The Festival of Britain was held in 1951. It was a great exhibition of what Britain had done in things like science, technology and design. Most people felt hopeful about the future. They were right to be hopeful. In the 1950s most people had jobs. They earned more than ever before. People spent their money on **consumer goods** like fridges and televisions, and on cars and holidays. A British Prime Minister, Harold Macmillan, told everybody, 'You've never had it so good.'

Most young people who left school at 15 found a job. They earned good money. They wanted freedom. They wanted to show that they were different from their parents. Their parents didn't always approve. Many young people spent their money on clothes, records, cigarettes and make-up. They went to **coffee bars**. There they drank coffee and listened to **rock-and-roll** music from the **juke-box**.

This is from the magazine Picture Pos Cheap holiday flights began in 1950. 1958 two million British people were having their holidays abroad.

Source F

This is a 1950s advertisement for Ford cars. Many people bought a car for the first time in the 1950s. This meant they could have picnics in the country and trips to the seaside.

Young people bought rock-and-roll records. They spent hours listening to them at home with their friends. They listened to American singers like Bill Haley and Elvis Presley, and to British singers like Tommy Steele and Cliff Richard. They **jived** to rock-and-roll groups and to **skiffle** groups. They went to rock-and-roll concerts and screamed when they heard their favourite singers.

The girls bought sloppy sweaters and trousers. They soaked their petticoats in sugar and water to make them stick out under their skirts. The boys wanted to look like pop stars and many of them tried to copy Elvis Presley's hair-style. Some boys wore long drape jackets, drainpipe trousers and shoes with thick soles. They were called **Teddy boys**.

Manufacturers realized that young people had a lot of money to spend. They began to design clothes and write magazines just for them. They began to make goods specially for them to buy. The word **teenager** was used for the first time.

Some people thought that they would have a better life abroad. Thousands of families left Britain to live in Canada, Australia and New Zealand.

Source H

How did things change?

1 Find the year in which each of these events happened:

- The Coronation of Queen Elizabeth II
- The first self-service shop opened in Croydon
- Cheap holiday flights began
- The Festival of Britain

Now put these in the order in which they happened.

2 People's lives changed quite a lot during the 1950s. Find **three** things which were very different in the 1950s from how they were in the 1940s. Make a big picture or write about the things which changed.

3 Not everything changed! Can you think of three things in people's lives which were the same in the 1950s as in the 1940s?

Tommy Steele often appeared on a TV programme called 'Six-Five Special'.

4 The 'swinging Sixties'

It is summer 1969. Robert is at the **pop festival** on the Isle of Wight. He is with his girlfriend, Linda. They are having a marvellous time listening to their favourite **groups** playing pop and rock music in the open air. Mum and Dad can't tell them to turn the sound down!

Robert is 22 and so is Linda. They were at **secondary modern school** together. Robert left school when he was 15. He went to **technical college** and trained to be a television engineer. He works for a local firm. One day he wants to have his own business. Linda works in a salon called 'Cut 'n' Curl' in the local **shopping precinct**. She is a hairdresser. They are saving up to get married.

Source A

This is a record album by the 'Rolling Stones'.

Source B

May is worried. She hopes Robert and Linda will be all right at the pop festival. Alison wanted to go too. Stan and May said 'No'. They said she was only 16 and that was too young. Alison was cross. Some girls in her class at the local **comprehensive school** were allowed to go. Stan and May miss Janet. She was always so sensible. She is a nurse now. Last year she married Bill Evans, a doctor. They live and work in Bradford, West Yorkshire.

May works as a school secretary in the local primary school. May and Stan can now afford to have holidays abroad. They are saving money in the **building society** for when they retire.

Source C

This is a record album by the Beatles. In 1965 the Beatles were given the MBE by the Queen. This was because they sold a lot of records abroad and earned money for Britain.

Linda and Robert at the 1969 Isle of Wight pop festival.

People call the 1960s the 'swinging sixties'. For many it was a time for fun and a chance to be different. Britain led the world in fashion, design and pop music. Fashion designers, like Mary Quant, used new fabrics such as **PVC** and **plastic**. They had new ideas about what clothes should look like. Furniture designers used materials like **perspex** and metal. New furniture looked simple and un-fussy. People liked bold swirly patterns in black and white, or in bright colours like pink, purple and orange. Tourists poured into London, where exciting things were happening.

Some young people wanted a different sort of life. They were interested in Eastern religions and ideas. They believed in peace and love. They thought that caring about people was more important than making money. These young people were called 'Hippies' or 'Flower children'.

Source D

This is a 1960s photograph of Mary Quant. She was a top British fashion designer. People all over the world bought her designs.

London was the fashion centre of the world. This was Carnaby Street, where people bought trendy clothes.

Source E

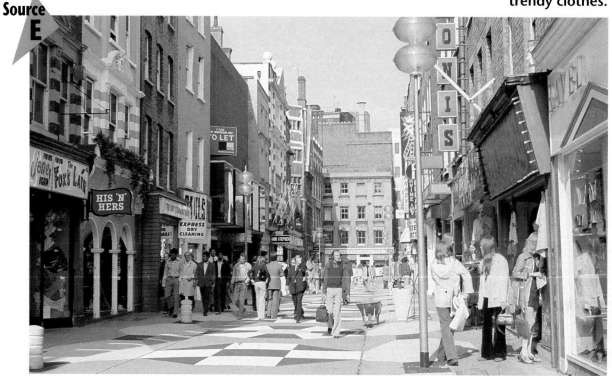

Television began showing programmes which made fun of anything which people thought was out of date. One of these programmes was called 'That Was The Week That Was'. 'Monty Python' was a crazy comedy programme which began in the 1960s. However, many people did not like this kind of thing at all. They preferred 'Coronation Street'. Huge numbers watched the broadcast on TV of Prince Charles being made the Prince of Wales. Plays shown in theatres were no longer **censored**. A play called 'Hair' shocked a lot of people because some actors were naked on the stage.

The Labour Government (1964–70) said that they wanted Britain to be a better place to live in. In 1965 Parliament said that no one should be **hanged** if they had murdered someone. Parliament passed laws, too, which let people live more the sort of lives they wanted to.

For many people the best thing that happened in the 1960s was when England won the football World Cup in 1966!

Source F

People often went on marches to protest against things they did not like. This is a photograph of a large demonstration in 1968 outside the American Embassy in London. People did not like American soldiers being sent to fight in Vietnam. In the 1950s and 1960s people joined CND (the Campaign for Nuclear Disarmament). They marched to protest against the nuclear bomb.

Source G

Me and my mates was really rooting for them. It was great when the final whistle went and then Bobby Moore held up the trophy. I felt proud to be English. I never thought England would win the World Cup.

Rob White remembers watching the World Cup on TV in 1966. England beat West Germany 4–2 in the final.

Activities

1 Lots of new and exciting things happened in the 'swinging sixties'. Look at Sources D and E. Read pages 32 and 33.

What things would young people like Robert and Linda have thought new and exciting? Make a list of these, or draw a picture showing as many of them as possible.

2 Source F shows people demonstrating against the war in Vietnam. If YOU were going to demonstrate against something today, what would this be?

Not everyone in the 1960s was 'swinging'. For some people the 1960s were a time of sadness and worry. Programmes on TV made people think more about world problems. People gave money to organizations like **Oxfam** which helped starving people overseas. They supported **Shelter**. This set up projects to make slums fit to live in, and kept asking the government to provide houses for all who needed them.

Slowly, people began to realize that **pollution** from industry could harm all living things now and in the future.

The **churches** wanted everybody to understand the **Christian** message. In 1961 the **New English Bible** was published in modern English. It was soon a **best-seller**. However, fewer people went to church in the 1960s than ever before. The only church which increased its membership was the Roman Catholic church.

In March 1967 the oil tanker *Torrey Canyon* was wrecked off the coast of Cornwall. Giant oil slicks polluted the sea and the beaches. Birds and fish were killed. People tried to help, but no one knew what to do.

In October 1966 a great tip of coal waste buried a primary school in the village of Aberfan in South Wales. 116 children and 28 adults were killed. The rescue attempt was shown on TV. People were shocked and upset. They sent money to the disaster fund.

In the 1950s and for most of the 1960s there was plenty of work. There were even jobs which could not be filled. London Transport asked people from the West Indies to come and help run the buses and the Underground. Hospitals asked people from India and Pakistan to come and work as doctors and nurses.

Anyone who was born in a **Commonwealth** country could come and live in Britain. Many Commonwealth immigrants settled in the Midlands and the north of England, as well as in London. They brought to Britain new sorts of food, clothes, music and religion. Yet they were sometimes badly treated because of their skin colour. People already living here did all kinds of things to stop them getting jobs, renting rooms and living ordinary lives.

In 1962 Parliament changed the law to make it harder for Asian, West Indian and African people to come and live in Britain. Some politicians even said that only White people should be allowed to come and live in England. A lot of people were afraid that there would be **race riots**. In 1965 and 1968 Parliament passed laws which said that everybody, no matter what their colour or race, must be treated equally.

Source J

Immigrants arriving to live and work in Britain.

What do people say about the past?

1 Matthew is 17. He is talking to his cousin Tracey. She is 13.

> 'The Sixties were really awful. I don't think much of the clothes, or groups like the Beatles. Did you know that a coal tip in Aberfan buried a primary school and killed 116 children in 1966? And that in 1967 a big oil tanker was wrecked and polluted the sea?

a What does Matthew think of the Sixties?
b What **information** is he giving Tracey about the Sixties?

Tracey says to Matthew:

> 'The Swinging Sixties were really good! The clothes were fantastic and the music was great! Didn't you know that England won the football World Cup in 1966? And that 'Coronation Street' started in the 1960s?'

c Why do you think Tracey does not agree with Matthew about the Sixties?

2 Tracey talks about 'the swinging sixties'. Read through this unit again. Can you think of another name to describe the Sixties?

5 The stormy Seventies

It is summer 1974. Janet and Bill have been married for six years. Their son Matthew is three. He goes to a **playgroup**. Janet and Bill are pleased that he will never have to learn about pounds, shillings and pence – only the new **decimal currenc**y. They all live in Bradford, West Yorkshire. Janet stopped work when Matthew was born. The local hospital sometimes asks her to help out when they are short of nurses. Bill works at a **health centre**. He is a family doctor. A lot of his patients are **Asian**.

Amar is one of Bill's patients. He is an **engineer**. Amar's parents chose a wife for him. This usually happens in **Muslim** families. They thought he would be happy with his cousin, Nasreen. Amar and Nasreen agreed. The families decided on a date.

Source A Janet at a Muslim wedding party.

The wedding was in Nasreen's house. Only the two families were there, with the **Imam** from the local **mosque**. The Imam read from the **Qur'an** and talked to Amar and Nasreen about marriage. Amar and Nasreen repeated three times that they wanted to marry each other. **Mahr** was paid to Nasreen and the marriage contract signed. The Imam blessed them, and asked **Allah** to bless them.

Amar and Nasreen then went to a marvellous party. All their relations and friends were there, including Bill and Janet. The men and women celebrated in separate rooms. Amar was the only man allowed to celebrate with his new wife and the other women. Janet hoped Bill was enjoying himself as much as she was! She wonders what Alison would make of it all. Alison has just finished studying at **Sussex University**. She has a degree in **Sociology** and wants to train to be a **social worker**.

Activities

Find Amar and Nasreen. They have just been married.

What is Amar wearing? What does he have round his neck?

What is Nasreen wearing? Look at Nasreen's hands. What can you see?

Are Nasreen's clothes different from what the other women are wearing? If so, how are they different?

British troops in Northern Ireland.

There were terrible problems in Northern Ireland. The **Catholics** felt they had no chance of a fair life. This was because most people in Northern Ireland were **Protestants.** They ran the Northern Ireland Parliament and the local councils. The police were Protestants. Protestants got more and better council houses and jobs. In 1968 groups of Catholics began to say that they wanted things to change. One of their leaders was 21-year-old Bernadette Devlin. The Catholics marched and held peaceful demonstrations. The police tried to make them stop. Fighting began.

In August 1969 the British government sent soldiers to Northern Ireland to keep order. The Catholics hoped the troops would help them. Later they believed they were helping the Protestants. Some Catholics belonged to the IRA (the Irish Republican Army) which wanted to drive the British out and re-unite the north of Ireland with the Catholic south. Militant Protestant groups like the UVF (Ulster Volunteer Force) wanted to keep Northern Ireland united with Britain and to smash the IRA. It was hard for people living in Ulster not to take sides. In 1971 the IRA began to bomb shops, pubs and stations in England. They wanted to force the British government to talk to them. The government refused – but it could not stop them either. The violence is still going on.

We will fight for justice. If it becomes necessary we will simply make it impossible for any unjust government to govern us.

Bernadette Devlin wrote this in 1969 when she was 21 years old. She was an MP at Westminster from 1969 to 1974.

A week ago, one of our section commanders was hit in the stomach by a sniper's bullet. The locals cheered at the time.

A soldier wrote this about his time in Northern Ireland.

There were different problems in the rest of Great Britain. In 1973 petrol and oil were hard to get and very expensive. This was because of a war in the **Middle East** between the Arabs and the Israelis. Most of Britain's oil came from there. At the same time coal miners went on strike. Petrol stations closed. Power stations could not produce enough power for factories, shops, offices and homes. Industries worked for three days a week instead of five. Most people had electricity black-outs.

North Sea oil was pumped ashore for the first time in 1975. This was British oil. This made more jobs for some people. Even so, there were still serious problems. The goods produced by British factories cost more than foreign ones. More and more foreign goods were imported. British factories closed down and a lot of people became unemployed. Many of those who had jobs said they weren't paid enough. Some went on **strike**.

Source E

Nurses went on strike in 1979.

Source F

We have seen the grave diggers refusing to bury the dead; we have seen rubbish piling up in the streets; we have seen schools shut in the faces of children.

Lord Hailsham, a Conservative politician, said this in 1979.

Activities

1 Who said what?
  Match the sayings with the people.

  'We want the British out of Ireland.'　　　The UVF

  'We want Northern Ireland to stay united with Britain.'　　　The IRA

2 Write a story about a nurse like Janet going on strike. Say why she did this. Use Source E and the information on page 40 to help you.

Many people thought it was unfair that some women who did the same work as men were paid less. Women, and men who agreed with them, went on marches and wrote to their MPs and to the newspapers. They demanded **equal rights** for men and women. The government agreed with them. In 1970 Parliament said that women must be paid the same money as men if they did the same work. This did not solve the problem. In 1975, 25 out of every 100 people who went out to work were women. They earned a great deal less than men. Very few women had top jobs.

In 1975 Parliament said that women had to have equal rights with men when it came to things like education, getting houses, getting jobs and buying goods in shops. The government set up an **Equal Opportunities Commission**. This found out what had happened when a man or a woman said they had been treated unfairly.

Source G

A lot of people were very angry that I went back to work. They said I was taking a job away from a man who might have a wife and children. They said I should stay at home and look after the baby. They said my husband should keep me.

Karen Lancaster, on getting a job in 1977.

Source H

Perhaps the most important work of all is motherhood. If the good Lord had intended us all having equal rights to go out to work and to behave equally, you know He really wouldn't have created man and woman.

A male MP said this in 1977.

A woman added this graffiti to a poster for a Fiat car.

Source I

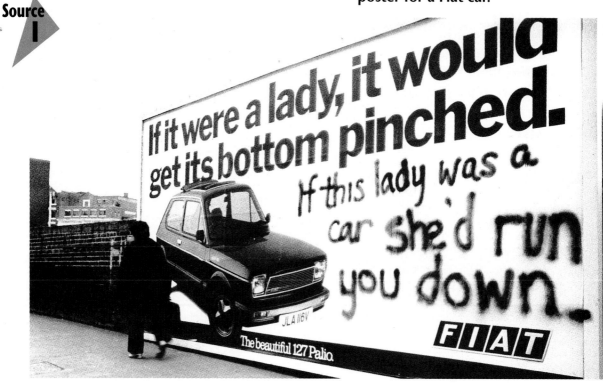

If it were a lady, it would get its bottom pinched.

If this lady was a car she'd run you down.

The beautiful 127 Palio.

FIAT

JLA 116V

There were some good times! In 1977 people celebrated the **Jubilee** of Queen Elizabeth II. She had been Queen for 25 years. There were services of thanksgiving, concerts and street parties. People rang church bells, held races, parades and carnivals. More than 100,000 people wrote letters to the Queen. In the same year Virginia Wade, a British tennis player, won the Women's Singles Championship at Wimbledon.

urce J

A Jubilee ice-cream carton.

Why did things happen?

1 Look at Source B on page 38. Why do you think the women are shouting at the soldiers?

2 Anne-Marie, on holiday from France, asks you why you say 'the stormy Seventies'. Use this list to help you explain.
   - *There were terrible problems in Northern Ireland.*
   - *Women and men went on marches to demand equal rights.*
   - *Lots of people did not have jobs.*
   - *Nurses went on strike.*

3 You tell Anne-Marie that there were some good times in the Seventies as well. She asks you to give one good reason for saying this. Which of these would you choose?
   - *Women gained equal rights with men in 1975.*
   - *People found oil underneath the North Sea. It was British oil!*
   - *In 1977 there was Elizabeth II's Jubilee. She had been Queen for 25 years.*
   - *Virginia Wade won the Women's Singles title at Wimbledon in 1977.*

Can you explain why you chose this?

4 Look again at the lists in Questions 2 and 3. These explain why Britain had good and bad times in the 1970s.
   Find: ONE reason to do with sport,
   TWO reasons to do with jobs.
   Why did you choose these?

6 The Eighties: time for change?

It is summer 1987. Alison and Gavin live in a large Victorian house with their children Emily aged four, and Ben who is one. The house is in Camden, London. When they bought the house it needed a lot of repairs. It now has a new kitchen and two new bathrooms. It has new **wiring** and new floor boards. It has a new roof, with **solar panels** to save electricity.

Alison is a **social worker**. She helps families who have problems. Gavin is a **journalist**. He writes for a newspaper. He goes abroad and sends back reports from trouble spots. Anne-Marie lives with them and looks after Emily and Ben.

Tomorrow will be May's 70th birthday. There is going to be a family party. Stan and May are staying with Alison and Gavin specially for the party. Stan and May now live in Herne Bay, Kent. They bought a bungalow there when Stan **retired**. Janet and Bill are now divorced. She and Matthew are coming by train from Bradford. Janet helps run one of the hospitals there. Matthew is sixteen. He loves football and rock music. He hopes his cousin Gary, who is fourteen, does too, otherwise it will be a pretty boring weekend. Robert and Linda are driving from Barnehurst with Gary, Tracey and Lisa. Tracey is twelve. She likes horse riding. Lisa is seven. She has ballet lessons. Robert now has his own radio, TV and video repair business.

Stan and May are proud of Janet, Robert and Alison. They wonder what the future holds for Matthew, Gary, Tracey, Lisa, Emily and Ben.

Activities

The picture on this page shows Gavin, Alison, their son Ben and Stan, his grandfather. They are in Gavin and Alison's kitchen in 1987.

Look back at page 5. Here are May and Stan in their kitchen in 1936.

Find as many differences as you can between these pictures. Look especially at:
– what people are wearing
– what people are doing
– what the kitchens looked like.

Do you think that Gavin and Alison's kitchen would be easier to work in than Stan and May's (page 5)? Explain your answer carefully.

▶ **Alison and Gavin in their kitchen with Stan and Ben.**

The Conservatives, with their leader **Margaret Thatcher**, won the General Election in 1979. A Conservative government was in power all through the 1980s. What they did then changed the lives of everybody in the country.

Mrs Thatcher said that the government was to be involved as little as possible in people's lives. It was important, she said, that people did things for themselves. This is called **private enterprise**. Mrs Thatcher was a very determined Prime Minister and she usually got her own way.

The government cut the amount of money they gave to local councils. They cut the amount of money they gave for spending on schools, roads and **nationalized** industries. They stopped prices rising. The government said that people could buy their council houses. They said that nationalized industries, like gas, had to be sold to people who wanted to buy a **share** in them. The government cut **income tax** so that people could spend their own money as they wanted.

Source B

Margaret Thatcher was Britain's first woman Prime Minister. This is part of what she said when she was elected in 1979: 'Where there is discord may we bring harmony. Where there is despair may we bring hope.'

Source C

At last we've a house of our own. After years of renting we can now afford to buy. We feel that we really belong here now. No one can tell us to leave. It's our house, not the landlord's.

Jack Lord said this in 1987 when he and his wife bought a house for the first time.

Source D

For every £1 I earned I used to pay 33p in income tax. Now I only have to pay 25p tax. I've earned the money. Why shouldn't I keep as much of it as I can?

James Murray said this in 1990.

The front cover of a women's magazine in August 1981. Prince Charles, the eldest son of Queen Elizabeth II, married Lady Diana Spencer in St Paul's cathedral on 29 July 1981. Huge crowds turned out to cheer them.

A year later their son, Prince William, was born. When Prince William was two years old, his brother Prince Henry (Harry) was born.

Activities

1 James Murray (Source D) used to pay 33p tax to the government out of every pound which he earned. He now pays 25p tax out of every pound which he earns. He earns £100 a week.

   How much money did he have left each week when he paid 33p in the pound tax?

   How much money does he have left now that he pays 25p in the pound tax?

2 Look at Source E. Why do you think the editor of the magazine decided to put this photograph on the front cover in August, 1981?

Information technology meant that good news and bad news were sent around the world very quickly.

The 1980s were not good years for some people. Many industries closed down or were in difficulties. In 1979 there were 1.3 million people unemployed. By 1983 there were over 3 million people out of work. Thousands of people, especially in the north of England, Scotland, Wales and Northern Ireland never found another job. There were riots in several large cities. Some people said this was because of unemployment.

There were other sorts of troubles, too. Many people were sad and worried by them. Many people were glad when the 1980s were over. They hoped that there were better times ahead.

Source G

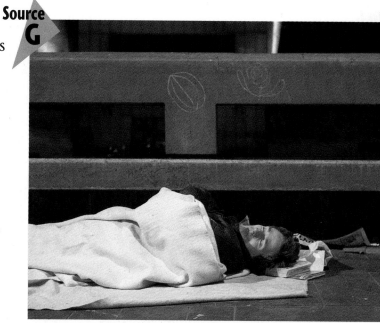

Hundreds of people slept rough on the streets of London and other British cities every night. Young people begged for money and food. Some people said it was their own fault they had no jobs and nowhere to live. Others said the government should do more to help.

Source H

On 11 May 1985 there was a terrible fire at the Bradford City football ground, where 51 people died. Football fans were also killed and hurt in violent accidents at the Hillsborough ground in Sheffield and at the Heysel stadium in Belgium.

Source I

It was April 1986. I was listening to the news on the radio. There had been a terrible accident in the Soviet Union. One of the nuclear reactors at Chernobyl had exploded. I knew what would happen. Clouds of radioactive gas would float over Europe. This would get into the rain which fell on the grass. The grass would be eaten by cows, sheep, reindeer and all kinds of animals. People who ate the meat and drank the milk from these animals could get cancer many years afterwards. I felt sad and depressed.

Sue Styles remembers in 1992 a radio broadcast she heard six years earlier.

There was famine in Africa. Men, women and children were dying. In 1985 Bob Geldof organized two huge rock concerts to raise money for them. The concerts took place in the USA and Britain at the same time. They were broadcast to 152 countries by the largest satellite link-up ever.

How do we know about the past?

1 a *'The Eighties were good years for some people.'*
Do you agree?
Use Sources C, D, E and F on pages 44 and 45 to help you to explain your answer.
b Choose ONE of these sources which you think **best** shows the 'good' side of the Eighties. Why have you chosen this? Why is it better than the other sources?

2 a *'The Eighties were bad years for some people.'*
Do you agree?
Use Sources G, H, I and J on pages 46 and 47 to help you to explain this.
b Choose ONE of these sources which you think **best** shows the 'bad' side of the Eighties. Why have you chosen this? Why is it better than the other sources?

OBSERVER/HARRIS

HOW HAS BRITAIN CHANGED OVER THE PAST 10 YEARS?

Richer	%48
Poorer	36
More freedom	44
Less freedom	24
More unhappy	48
Happier	21
More selfish	61
More generous	19

Opinion polls asked people what they thought. This poll was done by a firm called 'Harris' for the *Observer* newspaper in 1989.

7 Homes

Houses like this were built in the 1930s.

Activity

Look at Source A. This is a **semi-detached** house. There is another house just like this one joined to it.

Describe this house as carefully as you can. Don't forget the front garden, the garage and the gate!

Activity

Look at Source B. These are **terraced houses**. Describe the houses in the picture as carefully as you can.

A lot of new towns were built in the 1950s. Harlow, in Essex, was one of them. These are some of the houses that were built in Harlow.

In 1968 a gas explosion did this damage to a tower block of flats called Ronan Point in London. People were hurt and some were killed.

Tower blocks were built in the 1950s and 1960s. They did not use up much land. A lot of families could live in them. However, people living in tower blocks faced lots of problems.

Activity

Look at Source C. This is a **tower block of flats**. Lots of families lived here. Hundreds of tower blocks were built in Britain in the 1960s. Why did local councils think that tower blocks were a good idea? Think of the problems people who lived in tower blocks would have to cope with.

Old houses in the middle of cities were often pulled down. Shops, offices and even tower blocks were built where the old houses had been. In the 1970s and 1980s people decided to keep the old houses. They did a lot of work on them. People lived in them again. These houses are in the middle of Leeds.

How did things change?

1 Make a big picture which shows the different sorts of houses in this unit. If you can, describe how these are all different from each other.

2 Describe any ways in which the houses in Sources A, B, C and D are similar.

3 Some people moved into houses like these and their lives improved. Some people moved into houses like these and their lives became worse.

   Were things better or worse for people who moved into houses in Sources A, B, C and D?

8 Clothes

Activities

The clothes described in the list below all appear in the sources in this Unit. They are fashions from the 30s, 40s, 60s and 70s. Can you match the clothes to the date?
Make a grid:

Clothes	Source	Date

Enter the numbers on the list next to the sources they refer to. Put the dates in the last columns.

1 *A man wearing flared trousers.*
2 *A man with long hair, wearing a scarf and a wide belt over his hips.*
3 *A woman in a jacket with 'square' shoulders and a shortish skirt.*
4 *A woman wearing a long slim-fitting dress.*
5 *A man wearing shoes with platform soles.*
6 *A woman wearing a dress with a long, slim skirt.*
7 *A man in RAF uniform.*

Source C

Source D

Source E

Were things different then?

1 Look at Source A and Source E. Find as many differences as you can between the clothes in these two sources.

2 Now look at Source B and Source C. Both these photos were taken in the 1940s, but the women's clothes look different. Describe the different clothes which the women are wearing in the two photos.
Why do you think they are different?

3 Look back at the pictures in Unit 7. Fit the clothes in this Unit with the times the houses were built!

Source in Unit 7	Source in Unit 8
Source A – 1930s Source C – 1960s Source D – 1970s	

51

9 Spare time

Source A

Source C

Source B

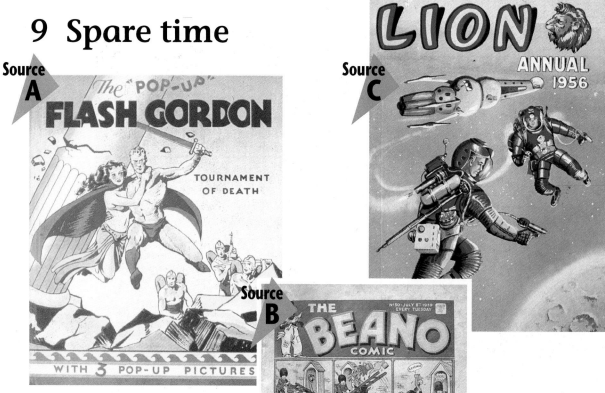

Children read books and comics like these in the 1930s, 1940s and 1950s.

Children queued to borrow books during the war.

Source D

TULSIDAS

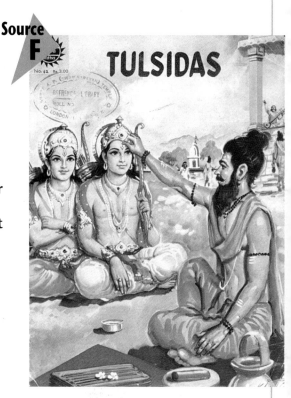

In the 1960s and 1970s magazines specially for teenagers were produced. There were magazines for children from Asia, Africa and the West Indies.

In 1967 a postal book club was started for children. It told them all about the latest paperbacks.

Some of the paperbacks available for children.

Activities

1 Do you read comics? Are they like the ones in Sources A, B and C? If they are, how are they similar? If they aren't, how are they different?

2 Do you borrow books from a library? What does your library look like? Is it like the travelling library in Source D?

3 Do you think that magazines like *Jackie* (Source E) and *Tulsidas* (Source F) were different from the comics in Sources A, B and C? How do you think they were different?

4 What are your favourite books? Have you read any of the ones in Source H?

Source I

In the 1930s almost half the people in Britain went to the cinema every week. They saw films like 'Top Hat' and 'Mickey Mouse'.

Source J

Source K

During the war most people listened to the wireless. They heard news of battles. They heard programmes like 'ITMA' and 'Music While You Work', which cheered them up.

Rhapsody

This teenager is listening to records on her own record player. Record players like this were made at the end of the 1950s.

Source M

People bought transistor radios in the 1960s. 'Trannies' were small and neat. They didn't have to be plugged in to a power socket. They worked off batteries.

A lot of teenagers listened to pop music. Many teenagers listened to Radio Caroline. This was a pirate radio station. It broadcast from a ship. It played pop music all the time.

Source N

This tiny television, 'Walkman' and CD player were made in the 1980s.

Activity

Look carefully at all the sources on these pages.

Which of these are **most** like things today? Which of these are **least** like things today?

Copy this grid into your book. Then write your answers in the grid. Explain your answers in the right-hand column.

Source	MOST like today	LEAST like today	Why I think this

People on holiday at the seaside in 1935.

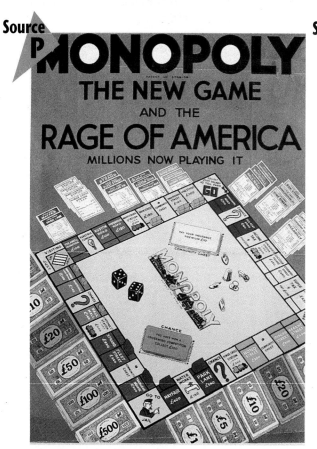

The board game 'Monopoly' came from the USA in the 1930s.

Meccano sets were often given to boys, and sometimes to girls.

Boys and girls had
'Chopper' bikes in
the 1970s.

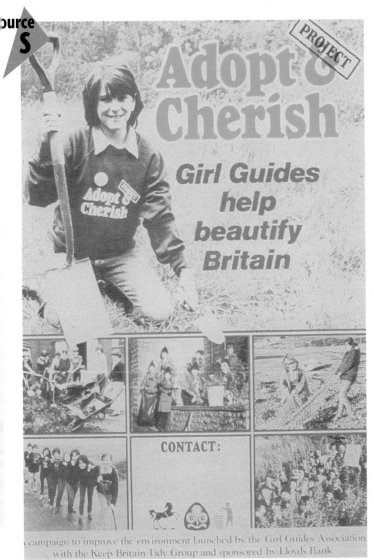

A campaign to improve the environment launched by the Girl Guides Association
with the Keep Britain Tidy Group and sponsored by Lloyds Bank

Girl Guides
helped protect
the environment
in the 1980s.

How did things change?

1 Look back at all the
   pictures in this Unit.
   a Find some things which
      changed between the
      1930s and the 1980s.
   b Find some things which
      stayed the same
      between the 1930s
      and the 1980s.

2 Look at the things you
   chose for question 1a.
   a Which of these changed
      a lot?
   b Which of these changed
      a little?

10 Getting about

Traffic on London Bridge in the 1930s.

Source **B**

Source **C**

Many city councils decided to stop using trams.

This woman is delivering milk in 1940. In some parts of Britain milk was delivered by horse and cart until the middle of the 1950s.

Activities

1 Look at Source A. What different sorts of vehicles can you see?

2 Now look at Source E. What differences can you spot between the vehicles in this picture and the ones in Source A?

3 Look at Source B. Source A shows that cars and vans were used in the 1930s. Why do you think horses were still used to pull milk-carts in the 1940s?

4 Source C shows 'Manchester's last tram'. A new tramway was opened in Manchester in 1992.
   a Lots of towns and cities got rid of their trams in the 1940s and 1950s. Can you suggest why they did this?
   b Why do you think Manchester city council decided to bring back trams in 1992?

5 Draw a big picture which shows how road transport changed between the 1930s and today.

**ource
D**

People bought cars like this in the 1970s.

**Source
E**

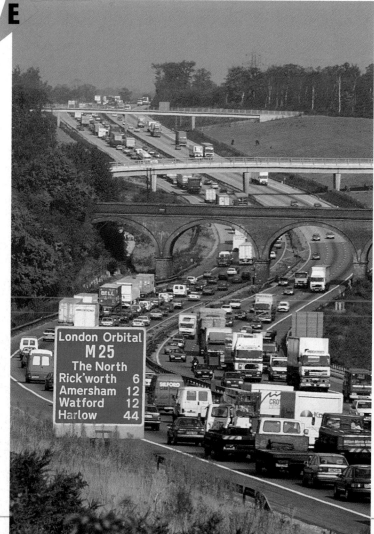

A busy motorway in the 1980s.

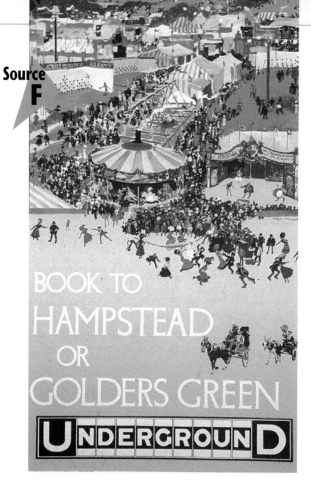

People saw these railway posters in the 1930s.

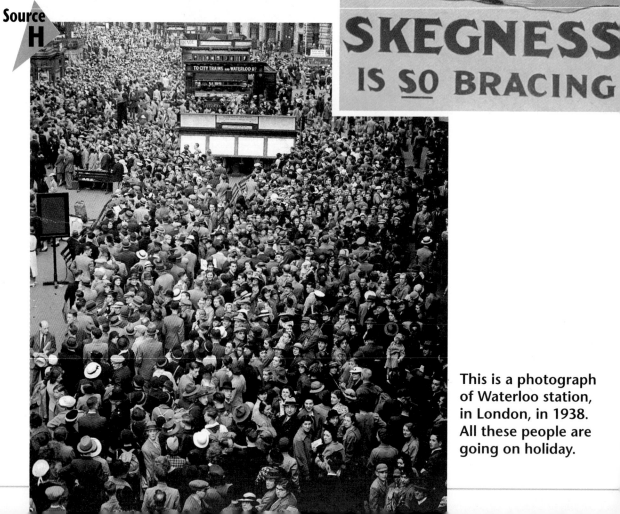

This is a photograph of Waterloo station, in London, in 1938. All these people are going on holiday.

A steam engine and carriages.

A '125' diesel express train.

Activity

Which trains do you think people would have used for these journeys? Put a tick in the right box. Use the sources to help you. You may tick more than one box for each journey.

Journey	Underground	Steam	Diesel
Going on holiday			
Travelling in London			
Travelling very long distances			

This is an Imperial Airways flying boat. From 1936 flying boats like this one flew to Africa, India, China and Australia as well as Europe.

Activities

1 Source L shows people getting on to a flying boat. Flying boats could take people to places aeroplanes could not. Why was this?

2 The *Queen Elizabeth* was 314 metres long. How long were Viking long-boats or 16th-century caravels?

Source L

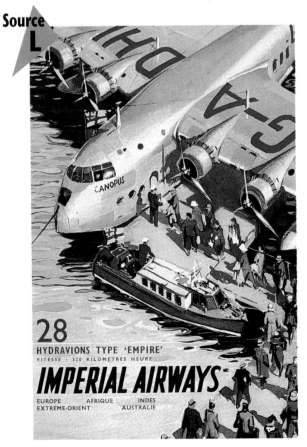

This is a 1930s poster advertising the flying boats.

Source M

This is the passenger ship the *Queen Elizabeth*. The *Queen Mary* was built in 1934 and the *Queen Elizabeth* in 1938. They were luxury ships. They carried passengers mainly between Britain and the USA.

Planes like this took people on holidays abroad in the 1950s.

3 Have you been in an aeroplane? Was it more like the one in Source N or the one in Source O? What differences can you find between the planes in Sources N and O?

Source
O

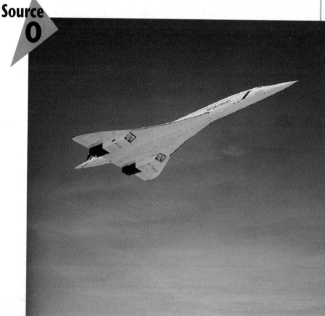

Concorde began making passenger flights in 1976.

How do we know about the past?

1 Look at Sources A, F, H, K, L and M.
Draw a picture, make a collage or write about 'How people travelled in the 1930s.'

2 Now look at Sources E, J, O and P.
Draw a picture, make a collage or write about 'How people travelled in the 1980s.'

3 'Cars, trains, boats and planes changed a lot between the 1930s and the 1980s.'
   a Which sources in this unit are most useful for proving this?
   b Why are they more useful than the other sources?

Source
P

A hovercraft at Dover in the 1980s.

INDEX

Conversion Chart

6d (sixpence) = 2.5p
1s 0d (a shilling) = 5p
10s 0d (ten shillings) = 50p
£1 0s 0d (240 old pence) = £1 (100 new pence)

Decimal coinage came in in 1971. Before then there were 12d in a shilling, and 20 shillings in a pound.

Comparisons: roughly speaking, sweets you could buy for 2d in the 1930s (such as a Mars bar) cost 6d in the 1960s, 6p in the 1970s and 20p by 1990.